MW00938155

BY THE WORD OF GOD

Tom Harmon

authorHOUSE®

AuthorHouse™
1663 Liberty Drive
Bloomington, IN 47403
www.authorhouse.com
Phone: 1-800-839-8640

First published by AuthorHouse 10/30/2010

ISBN: 978-1-4520-9609-4 (sc)

Library of Congress Control Number: 2010916039

Printed in the United States of America

Certain stock imagery © Thinkstock.

This book is printed on acid-free paper.

Edited by Bob English
Front Cover Photo by Steve McCormick
Proofed by Mary Evenson
Back Cover Photo by James Staddon

Ten of the items found in the front cover photo are metaphors found in scripture:

1. *The Milk Can – (I Pet. 2:2)*
2. *The Bread Tin – (Mt. 4:4)*
3. *The Bag of Wheat Seed – (Lk. 8:11)*
4. *The Lantern – (Ps.119:105)*
5. *The Sword – (Eph. 6:17)*
6. *The Frame of Honey – (Ps.19:10)*
7. *The Sledge Hammer – (Jer. 23:29)*
8. *My Mother's Bible – (Prov. 31:26-28)*
9. *The Level – (Eph. 2:20-22)*
10. *The Plumb Line – (Amos 7:7)*

Contents

Foreword:

This is my third book in a series of seven which I hope to write on the essentials of a consecrated life. I want to leave a legacy of faith for my family as well as the people God brings within my sphere of influence.

I want to especially dedicate this book to my precious wife, Joyce, who has been my faithful helper in God's Word. She has graciously listened to me work on Scripture memory. She has encouraged me and cautioned me as I've studied. We have shared the joys of digging deep and laying the foundation of our marriage and family on the Word of God. What a privilege to press on in the journey of faith with such a wonderful wife.

Preface:

The aim of this book is not to try and convince the skeptic or the scoffer that the Bible is the Word of God. It is only by the grace of God that anyone ever believes its divine revelation and authority. Instead, it is my desire to encourage those who have already been persuaded to press on and embrace its transforming power in their lives.

Chapter One:

Eternity

My Favorite Word

No word has affected the course of my life more than the word "eternity". The very meaning and purpose of my life find their significance in this single word. The values I hold for my marriage and family, from my work ethic to leisure, literally everything, comes under the influence of this one word. "For thus saith the high and lofty One who inhabiteth eternity, whose name is Holy: I dwell in the high and holy place, with him also who is of a contrite and humble spirit, to revive the spirit of the humble, and to revive the heart of the contrite ones" (Isa. 57:15). The concept of eternity is impossible to comprehend, yet the Bible has at its very core the issue of eternity. The Word of God begins with the bold statement, "In the beginning God." From the very first words in the Bible we are confronted with the claim that the God of the Bible existed before the beginning began.

"Lord, thou hast been our dwelling place in all generations. Before the mountains were brought forth, or ever you hadst formed the earth and the world, even from everlasting to everlasting, thou art God" (Ps. 90:1, 2). The concept of eternity had a profound effect on the man Moses, the penman of this inspired prayer. Because of eternity, Moses made choices that affected not only his life, but the lives of his family, the nation of Israel, and ultimately the world.

In the same text God moved Moses to write on the balancing issue; an issue we can all relate to, *the flight of time.* "The days of our years are threescore years and ten: and if by reason of strength, they are fourscore years, yet is their strength labor and sorrow: for it is soon cut off, and we fly away" (Ps. 90:10). Simply said, if you live to be 70 years old or 80 years old, life will go by in a blur. The Bible makes numerous references to the brevity of life. "Lord, make me to know mine end, and the measure

2

of my days, what it is, that I may know how frail I am. Behold, thou hast made my days as a handbreadth, and mine age is as nothing before thee, Verily every man at his very best state is altogether vanity. Selah. Surely every man walketh in a vain show: surely they are disquieted in vain: he heapeth up *riches*, and knoweth not who shall gather them. And now, Lord, what wait I for? My hope is in thee" (Ps. 39:4-7).

MY VERY BEST STATE

As I considered this Psalm of David I asked myself: "When was I at my very best state?" I was at my very best state physically when I was in college. I was playing football on a full ride athletic scholarship. I had big arms, a large neck, and massive calves with a 36 inch waist. Forty years have passed and everything has shrunk but my waist. Regardless of how much emphasis you put on the physical, it is an undeniable reality that physical life ends in death. Why would any reasonable thinking person want their goal in life to be a nice looking corpse at the end of 70 or 80 or even 100 years of life?

When were you at your best state intellectually? For me, I peaked at the age of 16. I'm not nearly as smart today as I was then. Seriously, when were you at your best state emotionally, socially, financially, relationally, spiritually, etc.? The point David is making in this Psalm is that if there is no eternity, everything is vanity. The word "vanity" means: it appears to have value, but in reality it has none. If all there is to life is time, and that goes by in a heartbeat, what is my reason for eating up food, drinking up water, breathing up air and taking up space.

"For what is your life? It is even a vapor that appeareth for a little time, and then vanisheth away" (Jas. 4:14). My father turns 84 next month and my father-in-law turns 90 this Saturday. Both are WWII veterans. My father drove a tank in the Battle of the Bulge. He was in the 10th armored division under General Patton's command. Joyce's dad was in the Navy and spent two years in the Pacific. In the past year we have helped both of them move. We had a great time as we came across old pictures of them in their uniforms. We saw pictures of them when we were small children with our grandparents. Now we are grandparents ourselves. Time goes by so swiftly even if you get your allotted 80 or 90 years, but what about the many that die before their time? What about the child that dies at birth, the 2 year old that is unexpectedly taken, or the teenager who dies in an automobile accident? None of us like to think about death, but it's the one reality that forces us to think about time and eternity. If there is no eternity, time alone is meaningless.

"Man that is born of woman is of few days, and full of trouble" (Job 14:1). In humble gratitude I must confess that my small sphere of life has had very little trouble. But as a citizen of the world I am forced to come to grips with the fact that the world is full of trouble. War, pestilence, disease, poverty, crime, pollution, corruption, hatred, prejudices, bigotry, threats, fears, death, betrayal, lies at every level, political, religious, home, school, work, etc. In this brief moment of time where does one turn to find truth? What is truth? "Heaven and earth shall pass away, but my words shall not pass away" (Mt. 24:35). The words of God found in the Bible are eternal and come from the perspective of eternity. Eternity is an issue of faith while time is an issue of sight. Living in time requires no faith at all, you can see its brief thumbprint everywhere you look. Faith always has to do with the unseen. "Now faith is the substance of things hoped for, and the evidence of things not seen" (Heb. 11:1). "But without faith it is impossible to please Him; for he that cometh to God must believe that he is, and that he is the rewarder of them that diligently seek him" (Heb. 11:6).

All of humanity lives by faith; the only difference is the object of their faith. All the religions of the world place their faith in something and hope it's true. Even the atheist who believes there is no God hopes it's true. Even those who don't know what to believe hope it's ok and live life as if it's true. Is the God of the Bible eternal? Is His Word eternally true? "He is the Rock, his work is perfect; for all his ways are justice; **a God of truth** and without iniquity, just and right is he." (Deut. 32:4). As one ponders the thought of eternity and faith he must come to the place where he determines what he believes to be his source of truth. As I've thought on time and eternity and distilled down the things of life and death, I've come to the conclusion that the Bible is the Word of God. It is completely trustworthy as divine truth. What sobers me is that all of eternity is dependent on that single conclusion.

ETERNAL LIFE

Francis DeSales (1567-1622) said, "You must form clearly in yourself the idea of eternity. Whoever thinks well on this, troubles himself little about what happens in these three or four moments of mortal life." My favorite word is "Eternity". It, like no other word, has helped me make sense out of time. The Bible is God's eternal Word, speaking clearly about the God of eternity and the whole issue of eternal life. The Scriptures speak repeatedly of eternal life. "My sheep hear my voice, and I know them, and they follow me. And I give unto them **eternal life**, and they shall never perish, neither shall any man pluck them out of my hand. My Father, who gave them to me is greater than all, and no man is able to pluck them out of my Father's hand. I and my Father are one" (Jn. 10:27-30). "And as Moses lifted up the serpent in the wilderness, even so must the Son of man be lifted up, that whosoever believeth in him should not perish, but have **eternal life**. For God so loved the world that he gave his only begotten Son, that whosoever believeth in him should not perish, but have everlasting life" (Jn. 3:14-16). "And this is **life eternal**, that they may know thee, the only true God, and Jesus Christ whom thou hast sent" (Jn. 17:3). "In hope of **eternal life**, which God, who cannot lie, promised before the world began" (Ti. 1:2). "For the wages of sin is death, but the gift of God is **eternal life** through Jesus Christ our Lord." (Rom. 6:23). "These things have I written unto you that believe on the name of the Son of God, that ye may know that ye have **eternal life**" (1Jn. 5:13). There are many other verses that speak clearly on the subject of eternal life. All the Scriptures are either directly or indirectly related to eternity and eternal life.

The Glorious Gospel

According to the Bible, the gift of eternal life comes through believing the message of the gospel. "And many other signs truly did Jesus in the presence of his disciples, which are not written in this book; But these are written, that ye might believe that Jesus is the Christ, the Son of God; and that believing ye might have life through his name" (Jn. 20:30, 31). "Being born again, not of corruptible seed, but of incorruptible, by the word of God which liveth and abideth forever. For all flesh is like grass, and the glory of man like the flower of grass. The grass withereth, and the flower falleth away. But the word of the Lord endureth forever. And this is the word which by the gospel is preached unto you" (1 Pet. 1:23-25).

What is the gospel? Let me lay some groundwork before presenting the gospel message. The gospel is entirely God's provision; I had nothing to do with it. Salvation is entirely God's provision; I have something to do with it--**believe it!** The gospel is not salvation. Salvation is what occurs when the gospel is believed, but the gospel is the gospel whether anyone believes it or not. There is only one gospel. "I marvel that ye are so soon removed from him that called you into the grace of Christ unto another gospel, which is not another; but there are some that trouble you and would pervert the gospel of Christ. But though we, or and angel from heaven, preach any other gospel unto you than that which we have preached unto you, let him be accursed. As we said before, so say I now again, if any man preach any other gospel unto you than that ye have received, let him be accursed" (Gal. 1:6-9). The apostle Paul makes it very clear that there is only one true gospel.

The gospel has everything to do with the righteousness of God. "For I am not ashamed of the gospel of Christ; for it is the power of God unto salvation to everyone that believeth; to the Jew first and also to the Greek. For in it is the righteousness of God revealed from faith to faith; as it is written, the just shall live by faith" (Rom. 1:16, 17). God's righteousness is reflected in the law because the law of God in the Ten Commandments demands perfection. One violation of one law made a person guilty of all, (see Jas. 2:10). Jesus did not come to destroy the law and the prophets but to fulfill them. Being made under the law, He fulfilled it perfectly, thus demonstrating God's righteousness. All of our attempts at perfect righteousness have failed under the law. Any honest person must admit that they have violated at least one of God's commands, either in thought or in deed. God's Word makes it clear that, "There is none righteous, no, not one" (Rom. 3:10). "But we are all as an unclean *thing*, and all our righteousnesses are as filthy rags; and we all do fade as a leaf, and our iniquities, like the wind, have taken us away" (Isa. 64:6). The gospel is to be proclaimed as a message of what God has done for us, not what we have done for Him. "Not by works of righteousness which we have done, but according to his mercy he has saved us, by the washing of regeneration, and renewing of the Holy Spirit" (Ti. 3:5).

The Riches Of His Grace

Probably the most concise and powerful gospel Scripture is found in Romans 3:21-28. Up to this point Paul has been describing man's condition under the law. He is utterly helpless and hopeless. There is no chance his good deeds will earn eternal life. "Therefore, by the deeds of the law there shall no flesh be justified in his sight; for by the law is the knowledge of sin" (Rom. 3:20). What a blessing from the Lord when one feels despair under the law. Under the law, my best day will not be good enough. The gospel is good news! Here it is! "But now the righteousness of God apart from the law is manifested, being witnessed by the law and the prophets, Even the righteousness of God which is by faith of Jesus Christ unto all and upon all them that believe; for there is no difference. For all have sinned and come short of the glory of God, being justified freely by his **grace** through the redemption that is in Christ Jesus, whom God hath set forth to be a propitiation through faith in his blood, to declare his righteousness for the remission of sins that are past, through the forbearance of God; To declare, I say at this time his righteousness, that he might be just and the justifier of him who believeth in Jesus. Where is boasting then? It is excluded. By what law? Of works? Nay, but by the law of faith. Therefore we conclude that a man is justified by faith apart from the deeds of the law" (Rom. 3:21-28). When a person hears the gospel message of salvation by grace, the Spirit of God begins to work in his heart and draw him to believe it. This is something no man can manufacture in himself. It is truly a work of divine grace. When a person understands the gospel (by divine revelation) and by grace believes it, God places upon him the righteousness of God in Christ Jesus.

"For he *(God the Father)*, hath made him *(God the Son)*, who knew no sin, to be sin for us that we might be made the righteousness of God in him" (2 Cor. 5:21).

Faith

How much faith does it take to receive the righteousness of God necessary for eternal life? If the grace of God has revealed the truth of the gospel, then faith as small as a grain of mustard seed will do. The gospel has everything to do with my sinfulness being exchanged for His righteousness. "That if thou shalt confess with thy mouth the Lord Jesus, and believe in thine heart that God has raised him from the dead, thou shalt be saved. For with the heart man believeth unto righteousness; and with the mouth confession is made unto salvation. For the Scripture saith, whosoever believeth on him shall not be ashamed. For there is no difference between the Jew and the Greek; for the same Lord over all is rich unto all that call upon him. For whosoever shall call upon the name of the Lord shall be saved" (Rom. 10:9-13).

Works

What about works? "For by grace are ye saved through faith; and that not of yourselves, it is the gift of God, not of works, lest any man should boast. For we are his workmanship, created in Christ Jesus unto good works, which God hath before ordained that we should walk in them" (Eph. 2:8-10). We are created UNTO good works not by them. "But to him that worketh not, but believeth on him that justifieth the ungodly, his faith is counted for righteousness" (Rom. 4:5). Eternity and eternal life is secured for me on the basis of the righteousness of God in Christ Jesus alone. If I am not eternally secure in His righteousness alone, then I am not secure at all. I am left to my feeble attempts to be as good as I can. The hope of heaven for many people is their good works. My hope of heaven is not in my good works, but only in the person and work of Christ Jesus alone. I find most people want heaven, but not everybody who wants heaven wants Christ. Instead they want some merit of their own, some pride of life that makes God obligated to grant them heaven. What a horrifying thought to do the best you can and find it's not good enough. "That at that time ye were without Christ, being aliens from the commonwealth of Israel, and strangers from the covenants of promise, having no hope, and without God in the world" (Eph. 2:12).

LIBERTY TO CHOOSE

I must make a choice, either I choose salvation by grace or I try to earn it by my works. It cannot be a combination of both. "Even so, then, at this present time also there is a remnant according to the election of grace. And if by grace, then it is no more of works; otherwise grace is no more grace. But if it be of works, then it is no more grace; otherwise work is no more work" (Rom. 11:5, 6). Jesus deals with this very clearly in the Sermon on the Mount. "Many will say to me in that day, Lord, Lord, have we not prophesied in thy name? And in thy name have cast out demons? And in thy name done many wonderful works? And then will I profess unto them, I never knew you; depart from me, ye that work iniquity" (Mt. 7:22, 23).

If I live until I am 65, and continue to preach at this present pace, I will have preached 10,000 sermons. I can't imagine standing before God and telling Him my hope of heaven is that I preached so many sermons in His name. The gospel of grace makes it very clear: my hope of eternal life better not be in what I do or don't do. If your hope of heaven is that you've spent half your natural life in a third world country serving tirelessly as a foreign missionary, then your righteous works would have been for nothing. If you worked hard and gave sacrificially to feed the poor and help the sick, even being involved in seeing people delivered of demons in Jesus' name as well as many other wonderful works for the cause of Christ, still your righteous works would have been for nothing. How horrifying to hear the Savior say, "I never knew you." The Father is known by those whose only hope is built on nothing less than Jesus' blood and righteousness. No merit of my own I claim but rest totally in the sufficiency of what God has done for me in the death of His Son on the cross of Calvary. "For Christ also hath once suffered for sins, the just for the unjust, _that he might bring us to_

13

<u>*God*</u>, being put to death in the flesh but made alive in the Spirit" (1 Pet. 3:18).

HIGH STAKES

By the grace of God I believe the Bible speaks the truth about eternity and eternal life. The stakes are high when you're talking about eternity. It's hard to imagine that in a frail moment of time our eternity is decided. Our life is but one grain of sand on the seashore of eternity. I pray all who read this think seriously on the meaning of "time" and "eternity". Eternity takes faith, time doesn't. "For he saith, I have heard thee in a time accepted, and in the day of salvation have I helped thee; behold now is the accepted time; behold now is the day of salvation" (2 Cor. 6:2). Remember the flight of time, from seconds to minutes, from minutes to hours, from hours to days, days to weeks; weeks to months, months to years, and years to decades. If God is revealing the truth of the gospel, I encourage you to stop and call out to Him for forgiveness of sins and receive the gift of His Son Jesus Christ. He is your only hope of eternal life. Tell God right now that you want Him in your life as Savior and Lord as promised in the Bible, the Word of God. May God bless you and give you a genuine hunger for His Word.

Chapter Two

Read It Daily

What a blessing it is to be able to read. Reading opens up a whole new dimension to learning. Until the age of twenty-one, I struggled with a reading disorder known as dyslexia. I had horrible reading skills even to the point of failing the fifth grade. I knew I wasn't stupid but I always felt stupid because I couldn't read. During my junior year of college I took a speed reading course that changed my reading ability. After that course I began seeing the words as they were written. As my comprehension began to improve, so did my confidence. I thank God for the many books He has allowed me to read, but the book that is at the top of the pile, hands down, is the Bible.

Solomon said, "of making many books there is no end" (Eccl.12:12). The printing press has dramatically accelerated the emphasis of his words. There are books written on every subject imaginable and even some unimaginable. There are magazines, newspapers, text books, novels, science fiction, documentaries, books on history, politics, math, geography, English, Spanish, French, etc. But of all the books in the world, the one that needs to be read more than any other is the Bible.

THE BIBLE AS A LION

The Bible is made up of 66 books, 39 in the Old Testament and 27 in the New Testament. "All scripture is given by inspiration of God, and is profitable for doctrine, for reproof, for correction, for instruction in righteousness, That the man of God may be perfect, thoroughly furnished unto all good works" (2 Tim. 3:16, 17). The Bible was written by God. God used holy men to write as they were moved by the Holy Spirit. "For the prophecy came not at any time by the will of man, but holy men of God spoke as they were moved by the Holy Spirit" (2 Pet. 1:21). God did not take away their personalities or their experiences, but neither did He leave it up to them to decide what was to be written in His Word. The authenticity of the Bible as the Word of God is constantly challenged. Many Christians try to persuade the skeptic of its divine origin. I wish to offer Spurgeon's short and simple approach in defending the Bible as the Word of God. "Defend the Bible as you would a lion, **just let it out.**" The remainder of this book will be just that -- letting it out.

ROADMAP FROM DEATH TO LIFE

The Bible is our roadmap on how to get from death to life. It's our instruction manual for living, from origin to destiny. The word "Bible" means, **the book.** No book is of value unless read. The Bible is no exception. If someone reads a book then they can tell another person what they have read, but someone must first read the book. When one begins to read the claims of God's Word, and is given faith by the author to believe them, the Bible will become an increasingly valuable treasure throughout life. The Bible is a book of *faith*. "So then faith cometh by hearing and hearing by the word of God" (Rom. 10:17). The Bible is a *living book*. "For the word of God is living, and powerful, and sharper than any two-edged sword, piercing even to the dividing asunder of soul and spirit, and of the joints and marrow, and is a discerner of the thoughts and intents of the heart" (Heb 4:12). The Bible is a book of *truth*. "Sanctify them through the truth; thy word is truth" (Jn. 17:17). The Bible tells the truth about the past, the present and the future. It is well worth reading.

DAILY BREAD

To the Christian, daily Bible reading is like daily bread. When the Lord Jesus was at the end of a forty day fast, Satan tried to get Him to turn some stones into bread. "But he answered and said, It is written, man shall not live by bread alone, but by every word that proceedeth out of the mouth of God" (Mt. 4:4). Jesus could have turned the stones into bread, but instead He made reference to the Scriptures, that the Scriptures come from the very mouth of God.

"Give us this day our daily bread" (Mt. 6:11). Most people eat at least once a day and usually two or three times. Just as our physical man needs daily nourishment so our spiritual man needs spiritual nourishment. Daily Bible reading is a means of nourishing our inner man.

NEVER UNDERESTIMATE
THE POWER OF A SERMON

In 1979 I heard a sermon about reading the word of God on a daily basis. The sermon was titled, "Read 'Til You Burn". It was based on the account of the two disciples on the road to Emmaus recorded in Luke 24. As the two traveled along, the resurrected Lord joined them, but they didn't recognize Him. They were temporarily blinded by God. Jesus perceived their sadness and asked what the problem was. They thought He must be a stranger in Jerusalem not to have heard about the crucifixion of the miracle Man Jesus. Many Jews had hoped He would be the promised Messiah and Deliverer of Israel. Then Jesus, beginning with Moses and all the prophets, opened up the Scriptures and expounded to them all the things concerning Himself. As they drew near to Emmaus, He was going to go on further, but they persuaded Him to come to their house and have a meal. As He blessed and broke the bread, their eyes were opened. They recognized Him. He vanished out of their sight, "And they said one to another, did not our heart burn within us while he talked with us along the way, and while he opened to us the scriptures?" (Luke 24:32) Every word Jesus spoke was in fact the living Word of God, yet He chose to reveal Himself as the real Messiah through the Old Testament Scripture.

Never underestimate the power of one sermon to change the course of your life. I had no idea of the monumental effect this message would have in my life. When a man preaches from the Word of God, it has the power to bring life to things that are dead. The hand of the Lord was upon the prophet Ezekiel and carried him out into a valley that was full of dry bones. There were a lot of bones and they were very dry. The Lord asked him if the bones could live. Humanly speaking he probably thought not, but he answered wisely and acknowledged the sovereign wisdom of the Almighty. Ezekiel knew only God could answer his own question. He was then commanded to preach to the bones and tell them to hear the Word of the Lord. The message was to contain a promise of life including tendons, flesh and skin, everything to make complete living bodies. So the prophet preached as he was commanded and first there was a noise, then a shaking and eventually the bones came together just as they were suppose to, bone to bone, with tendons, then flesh and finally skin. However, the completed bodies had no breath as had been promised by the Lord. The Lord had him preach some more. This time he was to preach to the wind. "Then said he unto me, Prophesy unto the wind, prophesy, son of man, and say to the wind, Thus saith the Lord God: Come from the four winds, O breath, and breathe upon these slain, that they may live. So I prophesied as he commanded me, and the breath came into them, and they lived, and they stood up upon their feet, an exceedingly great army" (Ezek. 37:9, 10). The valley of dry bones represented the whole house of Israel. They, like the dry bones, were dry spiritually. Their hope was lost and they felt cut off from God. Many people who have felt the same way have been brought to life by the power of the Word of God. "For the preaching of the cross is to them that perish foolishness; but unto us who are saved it is the power of God" (1 Cor. 1:18).

Establish A Good Habit

Immediately after hearing the taped sermon, "Read 'Til You Burn", I got on my knees and made a commitment to read my Bible every day for the rest of my life. The first week was great. I started in Genesis and never missed a day. The second week I managed about three days. The third week I never read it once. I was working a swing shift. One week I was on days, the next week I was on afternoons and the next week I was on midnights. I struggled for the next six months. Even when I did remember to read, five minutes later I couldn't tell you what I had just read. I asked the Lord to help me at least read my Bible through once in my lifetime. He began to help me by reminding me just before going to bed. Sometimes, He wouldn't remind me until I had already lain down, and then I would negotiate with Him about reading it twice on the next day. I began to understand that God wouldn't fall out of heaven if I didn't read my Bible that day. Eventually, I was reading more days than I was forgetting. "For I know whom I have believed and am persuaded that he is able to keep that which I have committed unto him against that day" (2 Tim. 1:12b). The Lord Himself was helping me establish a good habit in my life, a habit that would help establish me in my faith in Christ. "As ye have therefore received Christ Jesus the Lord, so walk ye in him, rooted and built up in him, and established in the faith, as ye have been taught, abounding with thanksgiving" (Col. 2:6, 7).

THE EFFECT ON YOUR FAMILY

In Deuteronomy, Moses gave instructions to the future kings of Israel on how they should run the kingdom. When he discussed the personal life of the king, he gave him instructions on how to govern with the right heart. A king needs protection from himself, protection from the dangers of authority. "And it shall be, when he sitteth upon the throne of his kingdom, that he shall write him a copy of this law in a book out of that which is before the priest and Levites; and it shall be with him, and he shall read therein **all the days of his life**, that he may learn to fear the Lord his God, and to keep all the words of this law and these statutes, to do them. That his heart be not lifted up above his brethren, and that he turn not aside from the commandment, to the right hand, or to the left; to the end that he may prolong his days in his kingdom, he, and his children, in the midst of Israel" (Deut. 17:18-20). The part that spoke the loudest to me is that his Scripture reading would affect not only himself but also his children. I knew I needed all the help I could get in being a better husband and father.

It took me a year and a half to read the Bible through for the first time. The day I read the last verse (Revelation 22:21), I remember the feeling of accomplishment and joy.

I wrote in the back of that Bible these words: "My soul wishes to write a symphony to God in which the entire Hallelujah chorus would be but an obscure half note." I hadn't studied anything or even looked at any of the study notes. I had just read the words of the Bible. It may seem like a bit of an over reaction to some, but to me it was truly a banner day experience. I hadn't planned on reading it again right away, but the die had been cast and my heart was set, so I started it again. I was falling in love with the Word of God and at the same time falling in love with the God of the Word. I was finding out that God is as good as His word and His word is as good as He is. His word is like a healing balm to my sin-ravaged soul, like a lamp to my feet and a light to my path. Bible reading has become like a refuge for me and a high tower from which I can see great distances on life's horizon. It has become like a fountain in which I can wash my mind from the impurities of this lower life. I would encourage all the redeemed of the Lord to make every effort toward daily Bible reading. I dare say that the benefits of daily reading will far outweigh the expenditures. It is truly a good habit and will help you get rid of some bad ones.

NEGLIGENT OR DILIGENT

Many people who are faithful church attendees and truly have a heart for the things of the Lord come to a place of "satisfaction" in their walk of faith. I think most people face the temptation to live off yesterday's grace. By that I mean, we are tempted to become complacent and satisfied with the things we already know and are established in. "Wherefore, I will not be negligent to put you always in remembrance of these things, though ye know them, and are established in the present truth. Yea, I think it fitting, as long as I am in this tabernacle, to stir you up by putting you in remembrance, Knowing that shortly I must put off this my tabernacle, even as our Lord Jesus Christ hath shown me. Moreover, I will endeavor that ye may be able, after my decease, to have these things always in remembrance" (2 Pet. 1:12-15). Peter made it clear that he didn't want to be negligent. The word "negligent" means "habitual omission of that which ought to be done, either by carelessness or design, inattentive to business or necessary concerns." Peter had already encouraged the readers to be diligent. A diligent person will not be distracted and will pursue with circumspection, accuracy and precision. This entire book will deal with things that most Christians already know but need to be reminded of and hopefully stirred to do. Daily Bible reading is no guarantee of a successful Christian life but it's truly a step in the right direction. Paul didn't hesitate to tell young Timothy to continue in the Scriptures that he had known since he was a child. Doing so would make him wise unto salvation through the faith which is in Christ Jesus.

What Saith The Scriptures?

In Matthew 21:23-27 it is recorded how the Pharisees had just challenged the authority by which Jesus was teaching in the temple. After Jesus settled that issue He began to teach in parables. The last parable in the chapter is known as "The Parable of the Householder". As Jesus spoke of gospel truths, He knew these supposedly learned religious men didn't get it. So He asked them a simple question. "Jesus saith unto them, Did ye never read in the scriptures, The stone which the builders rejected, the same is become the head of the corner; this is the Lord's doing, and it is marvelous in our eyes?" (Mt. 21:42). It would seem that Jesus is telling them if they were reading the Scriptures then they would have understood His words. What they didn't seem to understand was that Jesus, the One they were rejecting, was the very One upon which God was building. What stinging words to supposed theologians, "Have ye never read?" Reading and re-reading Scripture is a way God will reveal Himself to us.

The Blessing Of Reading And Hearing God's Voice

"Blessed is he that readeth, and they that hear the words of this prophecy, and keep those things which are written in it; for the time is at hand" (Rev. 1:3). Oh the blessings there are to those who read the Holy Scriptures.

25

It is like a balm of healing to a weary soul, like a flicker of light in a very dark world, like a helping hand when one feels all alone, like a caring look when one feels estranged, like a gift when everything around you seems so costly, and in the endless drone of man's advice, it's a haven where you can quietly hear from God. Oh blessed indeed, is he that readeth and they that hear the words of this prophecy.

Who Would Have Ever Dreamed?

There are few things that will bring and maintain freshness to your journey of faith like daily Bible reading. Learn to be creative. Read different translations. I have read all the familiar translations of the Bible and some not so familiar ones. I have read the Authorized King James, the New King James, the New International Version, New American Standard, The English Standard, the Amplified, the New Amplified, the Holman translation, Phillips translation, the New Living translation, the Living Bible, Good News for Modern man, the Message, and the American Patriots Bible. Currently, I am reading the Chronological Study Bible. The Bible I have read the most is the one I read through for the first time, the 1967 New Scofield Reference King James. It is my favorite simply because I have read it, studied and memorized from it the most. I am enjoying this part of my journey and am currently on my 51st time of reading the Bible through. Every long journey begins with the first step. As I look back now I say to myself, "Who would have ever dreamed?"

Chapter Three

Study It Carefully

"Study to show thyself approved unto God, a workman that needeth not to be ashamed, rightly dividing the word of truth" (2 Tim. 2:15).

Theology is the study of God. One of the most important facets of Theology is the fact that the Bible is God's Word of truth. One may accept the Bible as absolute truth yet fail to properly interpret it. Paul was concerned for Timothy that he would rightly divide the Word of truth. His words suggest that it is possible to wrongly divide the Word of truth. Our attempts to systematically organize and understand infinite truth is limited by our finite mind. Biblical theology is helpful, but not infallible. There are many good theologians, sound in the Christian faith, who study the Word of God and arrive at different conclusions. They may be wise and spiritual men but they're likewise trying to wrap their finite minds around infinite truths.

It makes sense to have a method of study. There should be certain rules you follow when you approach the study of Scripture. I have chosen to follow the seven laws of exegesis. I will list these seven rules and mention a few basic tools and resources.

#1. The Test of Words

The test of words would include: how a word is used in Scripture, how many times it is used, as well as careful examination of the definition, both in the original language and in English.

Strong's Comprehensive Concordance of the Bible, W.E. *Vines Expository Dictionary of New Testament Words*, Harris, Archer & Waltke *Theological Wordbook of the Old Testament*.

#2. The Test of Context

A study Bible and commentary. There are many good ones to choose from. The commentary I refer to the most is *Matthew Henry's Commentary.*

#3. The Test of Historical Background

Old Testament History by Charles Pfeiffer, *The Life and Times of Jesus the Messiah* by Alfred Edersheim. *Pictorial Bible Dictionary* by Merrill C. Tenney.

#4. The Test of Cross Reference

Thompson Chain Reference Bible, Dakes Annotated Reference Bible.

#5. The Test of Additional Examples

Today's Handbook of Bible Characters by E.M. Blairlock.

#6. The Test of Basic Concepts

Wayne Grudem's *Systematic Theology.*

#7. The Test of Good Fruits

"Wherefore by their fruits ye shall know them" (Mt. 7:20). At the conclusion of all Bible study one must ask the question, "Are the conclusions of my study producing the life of Christ in my life?" If so, they are approved of by God. If not, back to work and study some more.

Keep It Simple

"But I fear, lest by any means, as the serpent beguiled Eve through his craftiness, so your minds should be corrupted from the simplicity that is in Christ" (2 Cor. 11:3). There are few things as complicated as trying to keep something simple. A great help to me in this endeavor is to see all the truths of the Bible as they relate to the gospel. The gospel is directly related to every doctrine in Scripture. The gospel of Christ Jesus is the foundation on which every theological truth is built. Many of the moral principals and religious teachings of the Bible are within the range and understanding of the natural man. However, the glory of God's infinite wisdom shines through in the plan of man's redemption. This is, in my opinion, the theme of the Bible and can only be understood by divine revelation from the Holy Spirit of God.

The first step I take as I prepare to sit at my desk and study is to get on my knees and ask for the help and guidance of the Holy Spirit. I pray He would bring revelation of His holy Word and keep me from heresy. I acknowledge my absolute dependence on Him to teach me the things I need to know so I can grow in the grace and knowledge of the Lord Jesus. I humble myself before Him knowing that I have no wisdom to give Him because He is the very source of wisdom. "For the Jews require a sign, and the Greeks seek after wisdom; but we preach Christ crucified, unto the Jews a stumbling block, and unto the Gentiles foolishness; But unto them who are called, both Jews and Greeks, Christ the power of God and the wisdom of God. Because the foolishness of God is wiser than men; and the weakness of God is stronger than men. For you see your calling brethren, how that not many wise men after the flesh, not many mighty, not many noble, are called; but God hath chosen the foolish things of the world to confound the wise; and God hath chosen the weak things of the world to confound the things which are mighty; and the base things of the world and things which are despised, hath God chosen, yea, and things which are not, to bring to nothing things that are. That no flesh should glory in his presence. But of him are you in Christ Jesus, who of God is made unto us wisdom, and righteousness, and sanctification, and redemption; that, according as it is written, He that glorieth, let him glory in the Lord" (1 Cor. 1:22-31).

The Divine Teacher

Oh to be teachable. The Holy Spirit of God is the Teacher. The student is not the teacher. That may seem obvious but there are times I forget. Jesus referred to this when He said, "I have yet many things to say unto you, but you cannot bear them now. Nevertheless, when he, the Spirit of truth is come, he will guide you into all truth; for he shall not speak of himself, but whatever he shall hear, that shall he speak; and he will show you things to come. He shall glorify me; for he shall receive of mine, and shall show it unto you" (Jn. 16:12-14). The Holy Spirit is the Teacher. "But the anointing which you have received of him abideth in you, and you need not that any many teach you; but as that same anointing teacheth you of all things, and is truth, and is no lie, and even as it hath taught you, ye shall abide in him" (1 Jn. 2:27). This does not mean that we take spiritual teachers and throw them to the wind. No, God has given them to the church (see Eph. 4:11). Instead, we become like the church at Berea who searched the Scriptures daily to see whether the words of Paul were true (see Acts 17:11)

Choose A Topic

Ask the Lord what He would have you study. Wait on Him and see if He impresses anything on your heart. Ask Him to lead you in the way you should go. Maybe you have an interest already and just haven't begun the journey. Don't be in a hurry. Be willing to continue a year in your study. Gather some helpful books by trusted authors. Study one of the many attributes of God, e.g.. Creator,

Father, Holy, Righteous, Just, Judge, Merciful, etc. Study a topic, e.g. the authority of Scripture, end times, the church, Satan, angels, marriage, family, government, sin, depravity, heaven, hell, etc. Or choose a particular book of the Bible and spend a year studying it.

SET ASIDE A SPECIFIC TIME

When I first determined to study Scripture, I chose a two hour block, one day a week. The first subject I chose to study was the virgin birth of Jesus. I was taught to believe in the virgin birth but I had no clue why. Within a few months God had revealed to me the scriptural basis for this non-negotiable doctrine. Little did I know how this simple study would change my life and create a hunger in me for the study of Scripture. It wasn't long before I was teaching a Sunday school class. My two hours a week weren't nearly enough. I am convinced that the teacher benefits more than anyone in the class. The discipline of study soon becomes a delight. Soon you look forward to the times of seeking the Lord and the truth of His Word.

THE GREAT ADVANTAGE

Just having the Scriptures is no guarantee of salvation, but not having the Scriptures is a sure guarantee of damnation. When a person has access to the Scriptures, he is a giant step ahead of those who do not. When a person is blessed by hearing the Word of God preached and taught, he has a greater advantage of having God reveal the truth to him. "What advantage, then, hath the Jew? Or what profit is there of circumcision? Much every way, chiefly because unto them were committed the oracles of God" (Rom. 3:1, 2). It truly is a great advantage to have a Bible and sit under good teaching and preaching. However, until the Lord reveals divine truth, we remain like Saul of Tarsus -sincere, passionate and religious, but lost. "But I make known unto you brethren that the gospel which was preached by me is not after man. For I neither received it of man, neither was I taught it, but by revelation of Jesus Christ. For ye have heard of my manner of life in time past in the Jews religion, how that beyond measure I persecuted the church of God, and wasted it; And profited in the Jews religion above many my equals in mine own nation, being more exceedingly zealous of the traditions of my fathers. But when it pleased God, who separated me from my mother's womb, and called me by his grace, to reveal his son in me, that I might preach him among the Gentiles, immediately I conferred not with flesh and blood; Neither went I up to Jerusalem to them who were apostles before me, but I went into Arabia, and returned again to Damascus" (Gal. 1:11-17). Paul, being a Jew, had the great advantage of the Holy Scriptures. Nonetheless, it wasn't until the Lord revealed divine truth that he received the gift of eternal life. God uses men to do much of the teaching, but it is God who reveals the things that are otherwise hidden. "But if our gospel be hidden, it is hidden to them that are lost, In whom the god of this age hath blinded the minds of them who believe not, lest the light of the glorious gospel of Christ, who is the image of God, should shine unto them. For we preach not ourselves, but Christ Jesus the Lord, and ourselves your servants for Jesus' sake. For God, who commanded the light to shine out of darkness, hath shined in our hearts, to give the light of the knowledge of the glory of God in the face of Jesus Christ" (2 Cor. 4:3-6).

EXPECT REVELATION

When a person sincerely follows a reasonable plan of Bible study and genuinely desires to know truth, it is reasonable to expect God to reveal the truth to him. God is not playing some sort of cosmic game of hide and seek, where He enjoys withholding Himself from His creation. "That the God of our Lord Jesus Christ, the Father of glory, may give unto you the spirit of wisdom and revelation in the knowledge of him, the eyes of your understanding being enlightened; that you may know what is the hope of his calling, and what is the riches of the glory of his inheritance in the saints, and what is the exceeding greatness of his power toward us who believe, according to the working of his mighty power" (Eph 1:17-19). The study of Scripture moves you into a whole new realm of excitement as you anticipate God speaking to you about the things of eternal life. Your faith is greatly increased and grows exceedingly. "So, then, faith cometh by hearing, and hearing by the word of God" (Rom.10:17).

STANDING STRONG

As God begins to reveal Himself to you through the study of His Word you will become stronger in your faith. "As ye have therefore received Christ Jesus the Lord, so walk ye in him, rooted and built up in him and established in the faith, as ye have been taught, abounding with thanksgiving. Beware lest any man spoil you through philosophy and vain deceit, after the tradition of men, after the rudiments of the world and not after Christ" (Col. 2:6-8). As you grow strong in the Lord and the power of His might you will have the grace to be lovingly firm in what you believe. You will not be easily deceived or discouraged. "That we henceforth be no more children, tossed to and fro, and carried about by every wind of doctrine, by the sleight of men, and cunning craftiness, by which they lie in wait to deceive" (Eph. 4:14). As a man builds a theological house he can expect the stormy winds of opposition to blow; but if he digs deep and lays the foundation on the Rock, the very gates of hell will not prevail against him.

DEEP THINGS FROM GOD

"In that hour Jesus rejoiced in the Spirit, and said, I thank thee, O Father, Lord of heaven and earth, that thou hast hidden these things from the wise and prudent, and hast revealed them unto babes. Even so, Father; for so it seemed good in thy sight. All things are delivered to me of my Father, and no man knoweth who the Son is, but the Father; and who the Father is, but the Son, and he to whom the Son will reveal him. And he turned unto his disciples, and said privately, blessed are the eyes which see the things that you see. For I tell you that many prophets and kings have desired to see those things which ye see, and have not seen them; and to hear those things which ye hear, and have not heard them" (Lk.10:21-24). It always is an undeserving and least likely group that God chooses to reveal the deep things about Himself. Shepherds, fisherman, carpenters, servant girls and slaves are the lot from which He draws. When Jesus chose His disciples to whom He would entrust the world-wide ministry of the church, He didn't go to the rabbinical schools of theology in Jerusalem. Instead He went to the lowly hamlets and common people of Galilee. One does not have to hold a PhD for God to reveal deep truths to those who study. "But as it is written, eye hath not seen, nor ear heard, neither have entered into the heart of man, the things which God hath prepared for them that love him. But God hath revealed them unto us by his Spirit;

for the Spirit searcheth all things, yea, the deep things of God. For what man knoweth the things of a man, except the spirit of man which is in him? Even so the things of God knoweth no man, but the Spirit of God. Now we have received, not the spirit of the world, but the Spirit who is of God; that we might know the things that are freely given to us of God. Which things also we speak, not in the words which man's wisdom teacheth, but which the Holy Spirit teacheth, comparing spiritual things with spiritual. But the natural man receiveth not the things of the spirit of God; for they are foolishness unto him, neither can he know them, because they are spiritually discerned" (1 Cor. 2:9-14). As you study and pray, don't forget to ask Him to reveal the deep things.

SECRET THINGS

"The secret things belong unto the Lord our God; but those things which are revealed belong unto us and to our children forever, that we may do all the words of this law" (Dt. 29:29). The prophet Daniel knew God in heaven could reveal secrets. He refused to panic when Nebuchadnezzar threatened to kill all the wise men of Babylon if they did not tell him his dream and what it meant. Daniel and his three friends prayed in confident humility to see if God would reveal to them the secret of the King's dream. The Lord was merciful and revealed the dream. As Daniel stood before the king, he was asked how he had this wisdom which none of the other wise men had. In Daniel 2:28, he boldly proclaimed that there is a God in heaven who revealeth secrets. Oh that Christians who trust in the Lord God would go to Him in study and prayer, and ask Him to reveal the secrets--regardless of the problems we face in life whether physical, mental, emotional, relational, financial, etc. There is a God in heaven Who revealeth secrets. "Seek ye the Lord while he may be found, call upon him while he is near; Let the wicked forsake his way, and the unrighteous man his thoughts, and let him return unto the Lord, and he will have mercy upon him; and to our God; for he will abundantly pardon. For my thoughts are not your thoughts, neither are your ways my ways, saith the Lord. For as the heavens are higher than the earth, so are my ways higher than your ways, and my thoughts than your thoughts" (Isa. 55:6-9).

Chapter Four

Memorize It Intentionally

Oh the blessing of hiding God's Word in your heart! For much of my life I had heard that a Christian should memorize Scripture. I had even made a few attempts at it without much, if any, success. Within the second year of committing my life to Christ, a man by the name of Jack Wyrtzen came to our church and preached a powerful one point sermon: "Get the Word of God in you." He must have used a hundred Scriptures in his sermon and never once opened his Bible. This man was living what he preached. I was so moved that I determined to start memorizing Scripture. The first six months was a wash. I was so discouraged I was near the edge of scrapping the whole thing. I was working at a system that had been recommended to me and I just couldn't get it. I would get where I could say it like a parakeet but within 20 minutes it was gone. My wife was my sounding board. She would listen to me try to quote a verse. Sometimes I couldn't even remember the first word.

CRY OUT TO GOD

I cried out to God to help me. He heard my prayer and this is how He answered me. By this time in my journey I was regularly reading my Bible. The Lord impressed on my spirit that anytime I saw a verse while reading and thought I needed it or felt led of the Lord to memorize it, I would write the reference down in the front of my Bible. I would try to memorize one verse a week. If I didn't get the verse in one week I would just move on to the next one. It took! I began to get verses into my memory. I knew it was working for me. The Lord was helping me and I knew it. "Being confident of this very thing, that he who hath begun a good work in you will perform it until the day of Jesus Christ" (Phil. 1:6). I desired Scripture memory to become a serious priority for the rest of my life. I felt God was custom tailoring a plan so I could see some success in this adventure of faith. "Faithful is he that calleth you, who also will do it" (1 Th. 5:24).

SEEING THE LORD HELP

While I was a Michigan State Trooper I would work on my verse just before going to work. One time my partner and I were working a midnight shift and it was my turn to drive. Very soon after hitting the road, we arrested a drunk driver and were on our way to the jail when we saw another drunk driver coming our way. I turned around and pulled him over. After a series of sobriety tests, I determined he was drunk and told him he was under arrest. I put the cuffs on him and we headed back to the patrol car. After putting him in the back seat I reached over him to put the seat belt on him. He cleared his throat and I knew he was preparing to spit on me. I won't share all my thoughts, but I wasn't about to let that happen. Just before releasing my defensive tactics, the Lord brought my memory verse to mind. "Be not overcome by evil, but overcome evil with good" (Rom. 12:21). I was stunned that this verse should come to mind at such a time as this. I wasn't quite sure what to do but I knew I couldn't follow through with my original plan. I prayed and asked God to help me. The young man never spit, though he did begin to curse and swear. He gave me the usual threats but I ignored them and instead began to ask God how I was going to overcome the evil I felt by being good to this guy. This guy said he was going to sucker punch me when I removed his handcuffs. When we got to the jail, my partner processed his prisoner and then I took mine in. By this time he was very hostile and I wondered how this was going to work out. Without all the details of how a person is booked, I will just say whenever a prisoner is potentially violent, the last thing you do before closing the cell is take the handcuffs off. As I unlocked the first cuff he spun around and held his fist doubled up at me. I looked him in the eye and unlocked the second cuff. He was frothing in fury as I walked out of the cell and closed the door. He flew against the cell door and cursed me hoping someone would kill me. When he stopped shouting, I blessed him. I told him I hoped he would learn everything he was supposed to in this terrible situation. I told him I hoped the judge would be lenient and nothing like this would ever happen again in his life. My partner was somewhat shocked. A door was opened to witness when he asked me about my new behavior.

MAKING IT TO THE HEART

The young man bonded out of jail the next morning and went to his sister's house. He was too ashamed to go home and let his parents know he had been arrested for drunk driving. His sister was married and attended our church. She asked who had arrested him and he told her it was the State Police. She looked on his paperwork and saw my name. She had witnessed to her brother several times. When she told him that I went to her church, he said he had never met a man like me before. He came to church with her the next morning. I was somewhat in disbelief as I saw him come into the church building and sit on the far side of the sanctuary. The pastor preached the gospel and gave an invitation. The young man responded and came forward. After the service I made my way over to him and told him I was glad for him. I asked him if he remembered me and he said yes. He knew he was drunk, but he remembered how vulgar and rude he had been. He had done everything he could to get me going, but he knew he had been the loser in the battle. He said he had never met a man like me. Instantly I thought, "What if he had met me the week before Romans 12:21 was my memory verse?" I knew the Word had made it to my heart and kept me from sin. I have no idea how many times that verse has saved my bacon by keeping me from trying to overcome evil with more evil. You can only overcome evil with good. Trying to overcome evil with more evil just doesn't work. A small verse left a large impact. It has encouraged me to keep hiding God's Word in my heart.

MORE ENCOURAGEMENT

Within a few years we decided to home school our children. My wife would shoulder the majority of the academics if I would teach geography, the Bible (including

Scripture memory) and help in science. The Lord is so good. Teaching Scripture memory to our children moved me to an entirely new level. We memorized our first chapter together. Then we memorized the entire Sermon on the Mount. Our children loved the challenge and we began getting a family out of the deal. There was a unity we had never had before. We shared a common goal. We also found a new resource for conflict resolution. "For the word of God is living, and powerful, and sharper than any two-edged sword, piercing even to the dividing asunder of soul and spirit, and of the joints and marrow, and is a discerner of the thoughts and intents of the heart" (Heb.4:12). We finally memorized the whole book of James. We realized we could learn more than we originally thought. All our children are now grown and have families of their own. All of them memorize Scripture with their children. All of them would say that the benefits far outweigh the expenditures.

Is Scripture Memory Scriptural?

"Thy word have I hidden in mine heart, that I might not sin against thee" (Ps. 119:11). "Let the word of Christ dwell in you richly, in all wisdom teaching and admonishing one another, with psalms and hymns and spiritual songs singing with grace in your hearts to the Lord" (Col. 3:16). "If ye abide in me, and my words abide in you, ye shall ask what ye will, and it shall be done unto you" (Jn. 15:7). "I have written unto you, fathers, because ye have known him that is from the beginning. I have written unto you, young men, because ye are strong, and the word of God abideth in you, and ye have overcome the wicked one" (1 Jn. 2:14). "Thy words were found, and I did eat them, and thy word was unto me the joy and rejoicing of mine heart; for I am called by thy name, O Lord God of host" (Jer.15:16). There is a difference in being in the Word and getting the Word in you. Being in the Word is reading or studying. Getting the Word in you is memorizing and meditating. I feel like there is only so much room in a person. When you begin to fill your life with the Word of God, something has to go in order to make room for it. We know from Jeremiah's own testimony that he internalized the Word of God. When he said that he ate the Word of God, he was not making reference to literally eating a scroll. He was memorizing and meditating on God's Word. What saw him through some of the most difficult days of his ministry, was the fact that the Word of God was in him like a burning fire. He could not walk away from God's call on his life. "O Lord, thou hast deceived me, and I was deceived; thou art stronger than I, and hast prevailed; I am in derision daily, everyone mocketh me. For since I spoke, I cried out, I cried violence and spoil, because the word of the Lord was made a reproach unto me, and a derision, daily. Then I said, I will not make mention of him, nor speak anymore in his name. But his word was in mine heart like a burning fire shut up in my bones, and I was weary with forbearing, and I could not refrain" (Jer. 20:7-9). Christians face hard times. It's a fact! There is nothing like having the Word of God hidden in your heart to see you through those times.

Have A Plan

Having a plan means setting a goal. If you set a goal of memorizing one verse a month, at the end of the year you will know twelve verses you didn't know before. If you only bat 500, you will have six verses committed to memory. You may say, "That's not very many." In response to that I would say, "It's a whole lot better than nothing." If you memorized six verses in a year you could have all of Psalm 1 or Psalm 23. Those two chapters are powerhouses which could be used of the Lord to transform your mind and life. Endeavor to do something. You may be surprised. "Moreover, I will endeavor that ye may be able, after my decease, to have these things always in remembrance" (2 Pet.1:15). Do the best that you can, and let the Lord do with you what best pleases him.

Some Helpful Hints

Scripture memory is work. Some people pick it up easier than others but I don't know anyone that looks at it like a walk in the park. The first step in the process is to get the Word of God in your hands and open it up. You can't put it under your pillow and sleep on it and hope it comes in through osmosis. It just doesn't happen that way. You must open it up and read over the selected passage or verse. After you get the Word in your hands you want to get it into your head. Read it in phrases, read it and focus on each word. Once you think you have it in your head, say it out loud to someone. This always seems to take it a notch deeper into your long-term memory. The goal is to get it into your heart. This is something that requires the help of the Holy Spirit. It is a matter of depending upon the Lord to obey what you are memorizing. But before you get the Word of God in your heart, you have to get it into your hands, then your head, and eventually into your heart. Once a person has tasted the fruit of Scripture memory and sees the many benefits, he will want more.

I share this last thought because I have found it very helpful especially in memorizing large portions. Memorize from the Bible you read and study the most. When I first began memorizing I had the 1967 New Scofield Reference Edition in the King James translation. Though I have read and studied from many translations since then, the one I have in my hands the most is that one. Over the years it has been this old friend that I use for memory work. In the past six or seven years I have become so familiar with the pages that I can actually see the verses in my mind. It is a blessing to quote a chapter or even a book as I page through it in my mind. The Lord has definitely used this to help me in my preaching and I am thankful for it. I have purchased several of these editions. They are all laid out precisely the same. I have made mental photographs of those pages. Using the same version is something you might want to consider, depending on how serious you are about a lifetime of Scripture memory.

Someone once said, "If you memorize a verse of Scripture, you will learn a thought of God. If you memorize a chapter of Scripture, you will begin to learn how God thinks." I do know this: God is as good as His Word, and His Word is as good as He is. Scripture memory is good advice to anyone and especially to those who are serious about growing strong in their Christian faith.

Chapter Five

Meditate On It Continually

Much of the modern day concept of meditation carries with it the idea of emptying your mind of all thought. With an empty mind you are free from restraint, free to entertain whatever thought might come along. This is not the idea behind biblical meditation. To meditate on Scripture is to think deeply on the Word of God, to ponder and reflect. "I remember the days of old; I meditate on all thy works; I muse on the works of thy hands" (Ps. 143:5). To *muse* means to think deeply, meditate, ponder, reflect, etc. To *amuse* means to shy away from any deep thinking. With so many distractions it is so easy not to think about God or His Word. It is truly one of the great graces of God when one can employ the discipline of scriptural meditation. Truly, His grace is sufficient. "But whosoever looketh into the perfect law of liberty, and **continueth** in it, he being not a forgetful hearer but a doer of the work, this man shall be blessed in his deed" (Jas. 1:25).

How To Be Successful

"This book of the law shall not depart out of thy mouth, but thou shalt meditate therein day and night, that thou mayest observe to do all that is written therein; for then thou shalt make thy way prosperous, and then thou shalt have good **success**" (Josh. 1:8). At some point in the brief journey of life one needs to ask, "What is true success?" We know the opposite of success is failure but what value system do you use to determine which is which? When have I failed and when have I succeeded? Just one short verse of Scripture cuts through all the philosophical fat and gets to the essence of life; "For what is a man profited, if he shall gain the whole world, and lose his own soul? Or what shall a man give in exchange for his soul?" (Mt. 16:26). Think on it!

Prosperity

"Blessed is the man that walketh not in the counsel of the ungodly, nor standeth in the way of sinners, nor sitteth in the seat of the scornful. But his delight is in the law of the LORD; and in his law doth he meditate day and night. And he shall be like a tree planted by the rivers of water, that bringeth forth its fruit in its season; its leaf also shall not wither; and whatsoever he doeth shall **prosper.** The ungodly are not so, but are like the chaff which the wind driveth away. Therefore, the ungodly shall not stand in the judgment, nor sinners in the congregation of the righteous. For the LORD knoweth the way of the righteous; but the way of the ungodly shall perish" (Ps. 1:1-6). The fruit of a man's life bears evidence of what he is thinking about. If a man thinks about the things of Scriptures, his life will produce the blessings of Scriptures: love, joy, peace, long suffering, gentleness, goodness, faith, meekness and temperance. For as a man thinketh in his heart so is he.

Perfect Peace

Peace is not always the absence of turmoil. Many times it is an unexplainable calm in the midst of a raging storm. If I am going to be honest, storms are just plain a part of life. They come from any one of three sources: the world, the flesh or the devil and sometimes all three at once. Some come up suddenly and some you can see building a long way off. But regardless of the source, the frequency or the ferocity, there is a promise in Scripture that is worth knowing and meditating on. "Thou wilt keep him in **perfect peace**, whose mind is stayed on thee, because he trusteth in thee" (Isa. 26:3). "And the peace of God, which passeth all understanding, shall keep your hearts and minds through Christ Jesus" (Phil.4:7). When man constructs his own peace it will inevitably crumble under tension. Just look at world history and all the man-made peace agreements. As I consider my own life I see it again and again. When I set my affections on things above and not on things of the earth, my entire perspective changes and a peace comes that I know I could not have manufactured on my best day. Perfect peace comes from the Prince of Peace. No imposter can produce what only comes from God.

NEGLIGENCE OR DILIGENCE

Negligence is the habitual omission of the things which ought to be done, either by carelessness or design, inattentive to business or necessary concerns. The apostle Peter made these issues very clear in his second letter. "Wherefore I will not be **negligent** to put you always in remembrance of these things, though you know them, and are already established in the present truth" (2 Pet.1:12). He was reminding them of something they already knew, something they were already doing. The reason he was reminding them was because he knew the results of the fall. He lived it everyday. He knew from experience that part of the curse of sin upon the mind is that we remember what we should forget and forget what we should remember. In short he is saying, don't forget to remember!

Diligence is steady application in business of any kind, a constant effort to accomplish what is undertaken. "And beside this, giving all **diligence**, add to your faith virtue; and to virtue, knowledge; and to knowledge, self control; and to self control, patience; and to patience godliness; and to godliness, brotherly kindness; and to brotherly kindness, love. For if these things be in you, and abound, they shall make you that ye shall neither be barren nor unfruitful in the knowledge of our Lord Jesus Christ. But he that lacketh these things is blind and cannot see afar off, and hath forgotten that he was purged from his old sins. Wherefore the rather, brethren, give **diligence** to make your calling and election sure; for if you do these things, ye shall never fall" (2 Pet. 1:5-10). The health and wellbeing of our mind will determine, in large part, the health and wellbeing of our life. In Peter's first letter in the first chapter he addresses this very important issue of the mind.

GIRD UP THE LOINS OF YOUR MIND

"Wherefore gird up the loins of your mind, be sober, and hope to the end for the grace that is to be brought unto you at the revelation of Jesus Christ" (1 Pet. 1:13). Our contemporary western culture is lacking a word picture that the people had in Peter's day. To gird up your loins meant to control your garments by gathering up the long flowing folds of cloth that hung down near your feet. You would bring them up to your loins and tuck them into your waist belt so you could be free to run or move about quickly unencumbered. It is used figuratively of the mind meaning to control your thoughts so that in your decision making you won't be hindered or confused. Our minds are always thinking. Our minds have the capacity to have complete and detailed thoughts in a millisecond. These thoughts evidence themselves most often in our behavior. If the thoughts are wholesome and good, then our behavior will likewise be wholesome and good. There is a saying in connection with the Biblical teaching of sowing and reaping found in Galatians 6:7-9: "Be not deceived, God is not mocked, for whatsoever a man soweth, that shall he also reap. For he that soweth to his flesh shall of the flesh reap corruption; but he that soweth to the Spirit shall of the Spirit reap life everlasting. And let us not be weary in well doing; for in due season we shall reap, if we faint not."

> There is a saying that goes like this:
> If you sow a thought you reap a deed,
> Sow a deed and you reap a habit,
> Sow a habit you reap a character,
> Sow a character reap a destiny.

When you look at your thought life in this way, you see how important it is to manage it.

AN ICE CREAM CONE

A number of years ago as I had been studying and preaching from 1 Peter 1:13, I realized how important it was to guard my mind from careless or even idle thoughts. There were times when Joyce could read my face and tell I was far away in thought. Sometimes she would ask me what I was thinking about, "a penny for your thoughts". Sometimes my thoughts weren't worth a penny and I would just answer nothing. One evening we were on our way home from a speaking engagement and I asked her if she wanted an ice cream cone. She said yes and we got one at the next exit. Within a minute of my first lick I was off in thought. She quickly recognized my far away look and asked me what I was thinking about. Rather than shamefully keeping it secret I thought I would go ahead and tell her. I said I was wondering where we would hide if we were attacked by a foreign nation. She gave me a distant and somewhat puzzled look, and I quickly said, "If you think that is strange, let me tell you how I got there before I forget." She listened in amazement as I told her this story. My first thought was innocent enough – I wondered when ice cream was invented. There is no sin in that. But for no reason I know of, my question was quickly answered with a picture from "Fiddler on the

Roof". Tevye was leading his horse and milk cart up to a little cottage for a milk delivery. It was cold and I could remember seeing the cart jostle over the cobble stone street. When he knocked on the door a little old woman stuck out her container and when Tevye went to pour out the milk, it had become ice cream. Within a millisecond my mind went to the cobblestone street and I was hurled by thought to England. While in England my thoughts turned to Robin Hood. Why? I do not know, but when your mind is on this kind of path it doesn't have to make sense. My next thought was if Robin Hood would have had a machine gun, he could have cleaned out Sherwood Forest. I then thought a machine gun isn't much of a weapon against all the high tech smart bombs of today. My next thought was where we would hide if attacked by a foreign nation. That was when Joyce asked me what I was thinking. My mind had been ricocheting off one disjointed thought to another. If she hadn't spoken to me when she did, I wouldn't doubt I'd have soon been doing something in China!

ALWAYS THINKING

If the mind is always thinking, and our thoughts always affect our behavior, the next question should be, "What am I thinking?" "Keep thy heart with all diligence; for out of it are the issues of life" (Prov. 4:23). This brings us back to girding up the loins of our mind. Thoughts are constantly traveling through our mind. Some of the thoughts are seemingly harmless; e.g. the ice cream cone story. However, an unbridled mind is always in danger of a wrong thought that begins to lead us down a wrong path. There are paths in our mind, some traveled more frequently than others. If your mind travels down a path of good thoughts, your life will bear good fruit. The opposite is also true. If you travel down the path of evil thoughts, your actions will soon reveal it. The more you travel a thought path the wider it becomes: from a simple foot path, to a two tracker, to a gravel road, to a paved one. If traveled frequently enough it soon becomes a major highway and all our thought paths eventually drift toward it. God's desire and design for His people is that they learn to take every thought captive under the Lordship of Christ (see 2 Cor. 10:5). God wants our mind to travel down a highway of holiness for the glory of the Lord and the good of His children (see Isa. 35:8).

The Old Paths Of God

Our thoughts need to be of God. The best way for our thoughts to be turned toward God is by being in the Word of God. When we are busy getting into the Word and getting the Word of God in us, we don't have time for idle thoughts. Our minds are so bombarded by the things of this lower life, but if we have been raised with Christ, we need to learn how to set our affections on things above and not on the things of this world. "Thus saith the Lord, Stand in the ways, and see, and ask for the old paths, where is the good way, and walk in it, and ye shall find rest for your souls. But they said, We will not walk in it. Also, I set watchmen over you, saying, Hearken to the sound of the trumpet. But they said, we will not hearken" (Jer. 6:16, 17). The children of Israel had walked away from the God of their fathers. They no longer desired to walk in the old paths in which their fathers had walked with God. They made it clear that they didn't even want to hear anything that even remotely resembled the Word of God. Even when they heard it, they were determined not to obey it.

King David knew the importance of walking right paths in his thoughts. "The law of the Lord is perfect, converting the soul; the testimony of the Lord is sure, making wise the simple. The statutes of the Lord are right, rejoicing the heart; the commandment of the Lord is pure, enlightening the eyes. The fear of the Lord is clean, enduring forever; the ordinances of the Lord are true and righteous altogether. More to be desired are they than gold, yea, than much fine gold; sweeter also than honey and the honeycomb. Moreover, by them is thy servant warned; and in keeping of them there is great reward. Who can understand his errors? Cleanse thou me from secret faults. Keep back thy servant also from presumptuous sins, let them not have dominion over me. Then shall I be upright, and I shall be innocent from the great transgression. Let the words of my mouth and the meditation of my heart be acceptable in they sight, O Lord, my strength, and my redeemer" (Ps. 19:7-14). "He restoreth my soul; he leadeth me in the paths of righteousness for his name sake" (Ps. 23:3). "Show me thy ways, O Lord, teach me thy paths" (Ps. 25:4).

CUTTING NEW PATHS

All old paths were at one time new. There was a time in my life when I had never had an immoral thought. I had never seen pornography. I had never traveled down the path of lust and indecency. To my shame I have traveled those thought paths as well as the paths of greed, and worldly things, bitterness and pride. I can tell you those paths are much easier to merge onto than they are to exit off of. Just as the thoughts of Scripture were at one time new to me, they have become my old paths.

One of the great benefits of Scripture memory and meditation is the cleansing and renewing of your mind. "Now are ye clean through the word which I have spoken unto you" (Jn. 15:3). There have been times when my mind has felt like a garbage bucket for satanic waste. In times like those I have made it my practice to pick up my Bible, read, study, memorize and meditate. It is then I sense a cleansing like no fuller's soap could ever whiten. The more I traveled that path the less I traveled the other. "I beseech you therefore, brethren, by the mercies of God, that ye present your bodies a living sacrifice, holy, acceptable unto God, which is your reasonable service. And be not conformed to this world, but be ye transformed by the renewing of your mind, that ye may prove what is that good, and acceptable, and perfect will of God" (Rom. 12:1, 2). There is no sure understanding of the will of God apart from the Word of God. Oh how powerful is the Word of God. "For the word of God is living, and powerful, and sharper than any two-edged sword, piercing even to the dividing asunder of soul and spirit, and of the joints and marrow, and is a discerner of the thoughts and intents of the heart" (Heb.4:12). Only a fool thinks he can match wits with his own thoughts and come out on top. I must learn to think the thoughts of God. The thoughts of God are in His Holy Scripture. You cut new paths and wear them into old paths the more you read, study, memorize, meditate, share and obey.

Refuse To Receive Thoughts

"Casting down imaginations, and every high thing that exalts itself against the knowledge of God, and bringing into captivity every thought to the obedience of Christ" (2 Cor. 10:5). Not every thought you have is your own, some are placed there by the philosophies of the world we live in (see Col. 2:8). Some of them are lies placed there by Satan, the father of lies (see John 8:44). Some of them are nothing more than the imaginations of our own heart. "And God saw the wickedness of man was great in the earth, and that every imagination of the thoughts of his heart was only evil continually" (Gen. 6:5). How does one cast down an evil thought? When I recognize an evil thought in my mind I consciously refuse to receive it. I acknowledge that the thought neither glorifies God nor benefits me. For example, if I think someone has done me wrong and I am thinking thoughts of bitterness or revenge, I cast them down and bring into my mind thoughts of forgiveness based upon the great forgiveness I have received from the Lord. The following verses are ones I have memorized and recommend them to anyone who struggles with forgiveness: Psalms 130:4, Ephesians 4:32, Colossians 3:13, Matthew 6:12, Luke 23:34, 1 John 1:9, Ephesians 1:7.

In the struggle with lust, remember the greats: Samson, the strongest man; David, the bravest man; Solomon, the wisest man; and Judah, from whose line would come the Christ. Other verses include 1 Thessalonians 4:3-7, 1 Timothy 5:22, Colossians 3:1-5, Ephesians 4:30, Philippians 2:5-12, Romans 13:11-14, Acts 26:16-19. For many men lust is an often traveled path. You will need some big guns to help you get onto some new paths and stay there. Regardless of the arena, whether it is anger, greed, bitterness, or the like, the Scripture has new paths for you to walk in.

THINK ON THESE THINGS

"Finally, brethren, whatever things are true, whatever things are honest, whatever things are just, whatever things are pure, whatever things are lovely, whatever things are of good report; if there be any virtue, and if there be any praise, think on these things. Those things, which ye have both learned, and received, and heard, and seen in me, do, and the God of peace shall be with you" (Phil. 4:8, 9). The above verses are a great description of the Word of God. Meditate upon it daily and the God of peace and the peace of God will become yours.

CHAPTER SIX

SHARE IT LOVINGLY

Those who believe the Bible is true can't escape the clear instructions we have to share it with others both in word and in deed. Sometimes it seems so easy and sometimes it seems so hard. Our success is largely dependent upon our personal walk with the Lord. When our life isn't reflecting the truth of Scripture there seems little reason to share it. We need that sweet harmony between our walk and our talk that Paul described when he encouraged

Timothy to be an example of the believer in word and deed, in conversation and love, in spirit, in faith in purity, (1 Tim. 4:12). When Jesus went about doing good He combined His deeds with words. He shared the gospel of the kingdom of God with power. When He sent His disciples out, He sent them to do the same. One of the good evidences that the Spirit of God is dwelling in you is that you want to share the truths of God with others. Be assured though, all kinds of opposition will come. Some of the opposition will come from within, some from without, some from unseen forces and some that are very visible. Regardless of the opposition, the instruction remains clear, whether in a group or one-on-one, speak the truth in love to those God brings within your sphere of influence. "But speaking the truth in love, we may grow up into him in all things, who is the head, even Christ" (Eph. 4:15).

TRUTH

Truth by its very nature is offensive. "And this is life eternal, that they may know thee, the **only true** God, and Jesus Christ, whom thou hast sent" (Jn. 17:3). That statement alone is enough to start a fight with every other religion in the world. This means that all the other gods of the world are false gods, propagating false religions with false prophets. "Jesus saith unto him, I am the way, the truth, and the life, no man cometh unto the Father, but by me" (Jn. 14:6). Truth is offensive because it can be so divisive. Jesus made this clear in His teachings. "Think not that I am come to send peace on earth; I came not to send peace, but a sword" (Matt.10:34). We know that sword is the Sword of the Spirit, which is the Word of God, (see Eph. 6:17). If one embraces the truths of the Scripture, then the Scriptures must be shared. The truth must be shared without compromise or concession, yet with compassion.

COMPASSION

I fear I have preached some sermons with great passion but with little compassion. I know I have, for my dear loving wife has shared those very words with me. The moment she did I knew she was right but I felt desperate to defend myself, a good indicator I was wrong. Truth can be devastating even when shared with compassion, but when shared without compassion it makes the truth obscure and almost impossible to see. It's a frightening thing when the lack of love takes center stage and truth drifts into the shadows, sometimes never to be seen again. When I am guilty of this error, it is always the same culprits: pride and self righteousness. I have studied and read on humility. I have sought it with sincere desire. Yet, there are too many times it eludes me. Simply said, when I share the truth in love, it is always with a humble heart. When I share it without love it is always with an arrogant heart. Truth must be shared if the soul has any hope for freedom, and the best case scenario is when it is shared in love.

HE HUMBLED HIMSELF

Jesus is always our perfect example. We always do the best for ourselves when we look to Him, the Author and Finisher of our faith. "Let this mind be in you, which was also in Christ Jesus, Who, being in the form of God, thought it not robbery to be equal with God; but made of himself no reputation, and took upon him the form of a servant, and was made in the likeness of men; And being found in fashion as a man, he **humbled himself**, and became obedient unto death, even the death of the cross" (Phil. 2:5-8). Jesus gave us the option to either humble our self or allow him to do it. He would much rather that we take the initiave.

Jesus wanted to use Peter in the early church but Peter was full of pride. He had walked with Jesus on the Sea of Galilee. He had experienced the power of God. Peter declared that he would never deny Jesus; everyone else might, but not him. When Jesus told him he would deny him three times before the rooster crowed, Peter withstood His words saying that he would die first. "For whosoever exalteth himself shall be abased; and he that humbleth himself shall be exalted" (Lk.14:11). After the rooster crowed, Peter was humbled. Not long afterwards he was useable. He could share the truth with compassion.

Dependence Upon God

Humility is open and unashamed dependence upon God. Oh how I love independence, the very same junk Satan first used to tempt man. In all honesty, I know I am totally dependent on God, even for my next breath, my next heartbeat. On the contrary, God needs nothing. As the apostle Paul stood before the philosophers of Athens he humbly told them the truth. "Then Paul stood in the midst of Mars Hill, and said, Ye men of Athens, I perceive that in all things ye are very religious. For as I passed by, and beheld your devotions, I found an altar with this inscription, TO THE UNKNOWN GOD, Whom therefore ye ignorantly worship, him I declare unto you. God who made the world and all things in it, seeing that he is Lord of heaven and earth, dwelleth not in temples made with hands, neither is he worshiped with men's hands, as though he needed anything, seeing he giveth to all life, and breath, and all things" (Acts 17:22-25). God didn't even need Paul. As Paul's knowledge of God increased, so did his humility. A wise friend once said to me, "In light of who God is, the only proper response is humility." "Humble yourself in the sight of the Lord, and he shall lift you up" (Jas. 4:10). A proper view of God will do much to give a proper view of self which produces compassion from a heart of humility.

Truth's Power

1 Cor. 13 may be one of the most powerful and concise portions of Scripture on the subject of sharing the truth in love. "Though I speak with the tongues of men and of angels, and have not love, I am become as sounding brass or a tinkling cymbal. And though I have the gift of prophecy, and understand all mysteries, and all knowledge; and though I have faith to remove mountains, and have not love, I am nothing. And though I bestow all my goods to feed the poor, and though I give my body to be burned, and have not love, it profiteth me nothing. Love suffereth long, and is kind, love envies not, love vaunteth not itself, is not puffed up, doth not behave itself unseemly, seeketh not its own, is not easily provoked, thinketh no evil, rejoiceth not in iniquity, but rejoiceth in the truth; beareth all things, believeth all things, hopeth all things, endureth all things. Love never faileth; but whether there be prophesies, they shall be done away; whether there be tongues, they shall cease; whether there be knowledge, it shall vanish away. For we know in part, and we prophecy in part. But when that which is perfect is come, then that which is in part shall be done away. When I was a child, I spoke as a child, I understood as a child, I thought as a child; but when I became a man,

I put away childish things. For now we see in a mirror darkly; but then face to face; now I know in part, but then shall I know even as also I am known. And now abideth faith, hope, love, these three; but the greatest of these is love" (1 Cor. 13).

Avenues Of Service

Different people have different spiritual gifts, but regardless of the gift, all ministry must stay within the guidelines of love and truth. "Now the end of the commandment is love out of a pure heart, and of a good conscience, and of faith unfeigned" (1 Tim. 1:5). Remember that all men have faith but not all men have truth. What turns a man from darkness to light is faith in truth, the truth of the gospel. God equips His servants with different spiritual gifts to enable them for service. "Having then gifts differing according to the grace that is given to us, whether prophecy, let us prophesy according to the proportion of faith; Or ministry, let us wait on our ministering; or he that teacheth, on teaching; Or he that exhorteth, on exhortation; he that giveth, let him do it with liberality; he that ruleth, with diligence; he that showeth mercy, with cheerfulness" (Rom. 12:6-8). No one person has all the spiritual gifts and therefore no one person can meet all the spiritual needs or walk all the avenues of service. Regardless of the area of service God has equipped you for, the truth of the gospel must remain center stage. Whether we speak a kind word in Jesus' name, give a caring look, a listening ear, a gift, a helping hand, or even a cup of cold water in Jesus' name, it is for the glory of God in the hope of the gospel.

ALL CHRISTIANS HAVE A MINISTRY

One of the main reasons all Christians have a ministry is because all Christians are a ministry. "Therefore seeing we have this ministry, as we have received mercy we faint not" (2 Cor. 4:1). Christians are supposed to minister to all people, especially to those of the household of faith. We are suppose to let our conduct be as becometh the gospel of Christ, standing fast in one spirit, with one mind, striving together for the faith of the gospel. I have come to realize that the more I serve others the stronger my faith becomes. On October 31, 1983 I sensed the call of God on my life to preach. It wasn't long before I realized that I would benefit the most from this service. I have a better grip on the gospel now than when I first began preaching, but best of all it has a better grip on me. I have by no means arrived, but I have some clear direction in where I am going.

WARNING

As in all the service you hope to pursue, there are inevitably some things you need to avoid; that includes preaching as well as other avenues of ministry. Scripture always says it best. "Flee also youthful lusts, but follow after righteousness, faith, love, peace, with them that call on the Lord out of a pure heart. But foolish and unlearned questions avoid, knowing that they breed strifes. And the servant of the Lord must not strive, but be gentle unto all men, apt to teach, patient, in meekness instructing those that oppose them, if God perhaps will give them repentance to the acknowledging of the truth, and that they may recover themselves out of the snare of the devil, who are taken captive by him at his will." (2 Tim. 2:22-26). The more time you spend in the Scripture, the more obvious service becomes. God did not reconcile us to Himself so we could sit around and turn sour. "And all things are of God, who hath reconciled us to himself by Jesus Christ, and hath given to us the ministry of reconciliation, to wit, that God was in Christ, reconciling the world unto himself, not imputing their trespasses unto them, and hath committed unto us the word of reconciliation" (2 Cor. 5:18, 19). God always has our best interest in mind. He knows how much benefit we receive from serving. "I know the thoughts that I think toward you, saith the Lord, thoughts of peace, and not of evil, to give you an expected end" (Jer. 29:11). The ministry of Jesus was also characterized by serving. "And he said unto them, the kings of the Gentiles exercise lordship over them; and they that exercise authority upon them are called benefactors. But ye shall not be so; but he that is greatest among you shall be your younger; and he that is chief as he that doth serve. For which is greater, he that dineth, or he that serveth? Is not he that dineth? But I am among you as he that serveth" (Lk. 22:25-27). There is no higher calling than to serve the Lord in humility, and speak His truth in love.

Top Of The Pile

Once we hear the Word of the gospel and are born again, the Word of God becomes so important in our ongoing journey of faith. Each of the preceding chapters has represented essential building blocks for our spiritual growth. Before the final chapter, I wish to give a brief review of the chapter titles and some thoughts to consider with each. If you establish a daily Bible reading habit, there will be many benefits but you will probably only retain about 10% of what you read. If you develop some measure of study, you will probably retain about 25%. If you take seriously the discipline of Scripture memory, about 50%. If you learn to meditate on Scripture, about 80%. If you share some truth you have learned and speak the truth in love, you will retain 100%. We are not measured by how much we read, study, memorize, or meditate but in how much we share. It's another one of the paradoxes of Scripture: if you want to find yourself, lose yourself; if you want to become wise, become a fool; if you want to become strong, become weak; if you want to become rich, become poor; if you want to retain, give. "There is he that maketh himself rich, yet hath nothing; there is he that maketh himself poor, yet hath great riches" (Prov. 13:7). It should never be our aim to be a cistern where we just pool up knowledge, but rather a conduit where we share His grace and blessing with others. Knowledge for the sake of knowledge can be dangerous. It puffs us up and leads to an inevitable fall. A wise old man once said to me early on in my journey, "Don't strive to know a lot, just know a little, well."

CHAPTER SEVEN

OBEY IT PASSIONATELY

Passion isn't as difficult to *obtain* as it is to *maintain*. Most people who have wanted to lose weight have heard about a particular diet that melts the pounds off. They get all excited and begin their journey. Things go well at first and then they lose heart before they lose much weight. It's hard to maintain the passion. Losing weight is simple, it's just not easy. The part that's not easy is the *maintenance* of the passion to obey the rules of the diet. Most people who have a weight problem know if they would just cut back on the intake and add some exercise, they would begin to lose those extra pounds. A passionately preached sermon can move us to make commitments and set some good spiritual goals. We leave the sermon determinedly resolved to stay focused on the goal we have set. The first week is great, the second week about 50/50, the third week we're back to where we were. How can we get and *maintain* a passion to obey the Word of God?

THE POWER OF PASSION

King Saul was the first king of Israel. He was a tall, shy man from the small tribe of Benjamin. When he was installed as king, he was reluctant to step up to the plate and assume his responsibilities. Therefore, some despised him and cast doubt on his ability to lead the nation. In 1 Samuel 11, Nahash of the Ammonites encamped in Jabesh-gilead and offered to make a covenant with Israel. The conditions required not only that the Israelites would serve the Ammonites, but also they would agree to have the right eyes of all the adult men blinded. News of this reached the ears of Saul and this was his response; "Then came the messengers to Gibeah of Saul, and told the tidings in the hearing of the people; and all the people lifted up their voices, and wept. And, behold, Saul came after the herd out of the field; and Saul said, what aileth the people that they weep? And they told him the tidings of the men of Jabesh. And the Spirit of God came upon Saul when he heard those tidings, and his anger was kindled greatly. And he took a yoke of oxen, and hewed them in pieces, and sent them throughout all the borders of Israel by the hands of messengers, saying, whosoever cometh not forth after Saul and after Samuel, so shall it be done unto his oxen. And the fear of the Lord fell on the people, and they came out with one consent" (1 Sam.11:4-7). The next day Saul made hash of the Ammonites and all the people were glad to establish him as their king. He passionately led Israel to victory and the people had no problem following his leadership.

To Obey Is Better Than Sacrifice

This same king a few chapters later was given instructions by Samuel to slay all the Amalekites including all the livestock. Saul only partially obeyed, sparing the king and the best of the cattle and flocks. The prophet Samuel was to come and offer a sacrifice and lead the people in worship at the victory God had given them. Samuel's arrival was a little later than expected and the men became anxious to get home to their families. King Saul took it upon himself to offer the sacrifice instead of waiting for Samuel. This was something that was totally forbidden. Samuel arrived at the conclusion of the ceremony and harshly rebuked Saul for his incomplete obedience. "And Samuel said, hath the Lord as great delight in burnt offerings and sacrifices, as in obeying the voice of the Lord? Behold, to obey is better than sacrifice, and to hearken than the fat of rams, for rebellion is as the sin of witchcraft, and stubbornness is as the sin of idolatry. Because thou hast rejected the word of the Lord, he hath also rejected thee from being king" (1 Sam. 15:22, 23). When Saul began to be hesitant he caved in to the voice of the people and compromised his obedience to the Word of the Lord. If he had been passionate to fully obey the Word of the Lord, the people would have followed him. When a man loses his passion, he compromises his ability to fully obey the Word of the Lord.

What Is Passion?

"Know ye not that to whom ye yield yourselves servants to obey, his servants ye are whom ye obey, whether of sin unto death, or of obedience unto righteousness? But God be thanked, whereas ye were the servants of sin, **ye have obeyed from the heart** that form of doctrine which was delivered you" (Rom. 6:16, 17). Obedience that comes from the heart is real passion. If a man can maintain his heart relationship with the Lord, he will have less trouble with disobeying His Word. The heart refers to the centermost part of our being, the inner sanctuary of our spirit and soul. It is that part of us that most concerns God. "For the Lord seeth not as a man seeth; for man looketh on the outward appearance, but the Lord looketh on the heart" (1 Sam. 16:7b). God sought for a man after his own heart and chose David to be king after Saul. David had a heart relationship of obedience with God. When David disobeyed (and he did), he knew it would mean broken fellowship with God in his heart. "One thing have I desired of the Lord, that will I seek after; that I may dwell in the house of the Lord all the days of my life, to behold the beauty of the Lord, and to inquire in his temple" (Ps. 27:4). Inevitably David would cry out, "Purge me with hyssop, and I shall be clean; wash me and I shall be whiter than snow. … Create in me a clean heart, O God; and renew a right spirit within me" (Ps. 51:7, 10). If our hearts are right with God we are more likely to fully obey and be passionate in our obedience. The apostle Paul acknowledged the struggle we all face; "For I know that in me (that is in my flesh) dwelleth no good thing; for to will is present with me; but how to perform that which is good I find not" (Rom. 7:18). What benefit is there in having the "how to" when you have no heart to use it? "Why is there a price in the hand of a fool to get wisdom, seeing he hath no heart to it?" (Prov. 17:16).

Passion, Truth And Trust

A man's conversation, his countenance and his conduct will eventually reveal what is in his heart. The simple truth is that I will not obey what my heart does not fully believe. I will obey things that I do not fully understand, if with my heart I trust the one who said it. "Trust in the Lord with all thine heart, and lean not on thy own understanding. In all thy ways acknowledge him, and he shall direct thy paths" (Prov. 3:5, 6). I have come to the place in my journey of faith where my heart is fixed on trusting the Word of God to be, in fact, **the** Word of God. I believe that God is as good as His Word and His Word is as good as He is. It is absolute truth as He is absolute truth. All the truth I will ever need or want can be found within the trustworthy pages of the Bible. Is this to say that I understand all the truth contained in its pages? NO! But the parts that I do understand I desire to obey knowing that the result will be for His glory and my good. "Trust in the Lord, and do good; so shalt thou dwell in the land, and verily thou shalt be fed. Delight thyself also in the Lord, and he shall give thee the desires of thine heart. Commit thy way unto the Lord; trust also in him; and he shall bring it to pass" (Ps. 37:3-5).

Everyone trusts someone or something, the question is who or what. "It is better to trust in the Lord than to put confidence in man. It is better to trust in the Lord than to put confidence in princes" (Ps. 118:8, 9). What governor or government has ever proven itself to be totally honest and trustworthy? If we can't trust others, perhaps we should trust ourselves? "He that trusteth his own heart is a fool" (Prov. 28:26a) I have proved that too many times. How about money? "He that trusteth in his riches shall fall" (Prov. 11:28a). I have lived long enough to see that played out many times among the rich and famous. The question must be asked, "What can I passionately trust as truth?' My answer is simple and firm--God and His Holy Word!

Passion In The Pulpit

Over the years that I have been preaching the Word, I have received numerous criticisms; most, if not all, have some element of truth to them. One thing I have never been criticized for is a lack of passion. As I preach the glorious gospel, many times I become overwhelmed with the greatness of the message; to contemplate the goodness of God to man really makes me passionate. After one such message a man came up to me and said he didn't believe a word I said, but he thought I did. I remember saying to him, "Hallelujah, I don't want you leaving here wondering if I believe it or not." My passion for what I believe to be the truth left him troubled. I am sure he did not feel equally passionate for what he believed not to be true. It would be a fearful thing to me to treat the living Word of God as though it were a lifeless book, worthy only of collecting dust on some distant shelf.

The Problem Of Passion

The heart that trusts the Lord and His Word can also be easily deceived and trust in itself. "The heart is deceitful above all things and desperately wicked; who can know it? I the Lord search the heart, I test the conscience even to give every man according to his ways, and according to the fruit of his doings" (Jer. 17:9, 10). Sin has so affected the heart of man that he must beware of its seductive capacities. The heart of man alone is no match for the seductiveness of sin. It is possible to be passionate about a lie, even a known lie. It happens in the world all the time and it can happen in the heart of a believer. The color of the heart hasn't changed since the fall. "And God saw that the wickedness of man was great in the earth, and that every imagination of the thoughts of his heart was only evil continually" (Gen. 6:5). It's not a very pretty picture, but one we must concern ourselves with if we are going to avoid the problem of passion just for the sake of passion. "Search me, O God, and know my heart; try me, and know my thoughts; and see if there be any wicked way in me, and lead me in the way everlasting" (Ps. 139:23, 24). Regular heart examinations are not optional. We are still vulnerable to the deceitfulness of sin, the pull of the world and the lies of the devil. If I am ever to experience the power of obeying the Word of God passionately, I must humbly acknowledge my absolute dependence upon God.

A Closing Thought

If you lack the passion to obey what you know to be the truth, here is a heart changer "And whatever ye do, do it heartily as to the Lord and not unto men" (Col. 3:23). Pleasing God is much easier than pleasing men. If you seek to be a men pleaser you will run the risk of displeasing God. If you please God, it doesn't matter who you offend. If you offend God, it doesn't matter who you please. We must go vertical first, and if the vertical gets right then He makes the horizontal right. "When a man's ways please the Lord, he maketh even his enemies to be at peace with him" (Prov.16:7). A life of faith and passionate obedience to Him is one focused on pleasing Him first. "But without faith it is impossible to please him: for he that cometh to God must believe that He is, and He is a rewarder of them that diligently seek Him" (Heb. 11:6).

May we all walk with the Lord
in the light of His Word.

LaVergne, TN USA
16 November 2010
205011LV00001B/2/P